I0160112

BIBLE VISUALS international

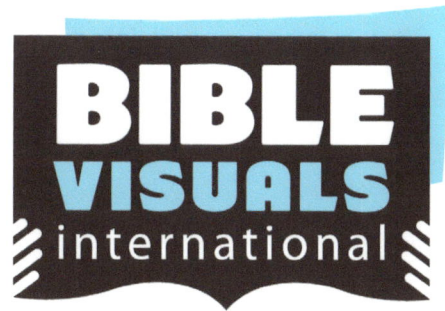

Helping Children See Jesus

ISBN: 978-1-64104-131-7

End Of The Spear,

Walking God's Trail Edition
© *2005 by Steve Saint, English US edition*

© 2020 by Bible Visuals International
with permission of Tyndale House Publishers
Project Development and Supervision: Karen E. Weitzel
Authors: Bryan Willoughby and Dr. Elaine Huber
Editors: Edie Cunningham, Lindsay Mayer Spreadbury, Karen E. Weiztel
Artist: Debby Saint
Computer Graphic Artist: Yuko Willoughby
Page Layout: Patricia Pope

Bible Visuals International
PO Box 153, Akron, PA 17501-0153
Phone: (717) 859-1131
www.biblevisuals.org

RELATED ITEMS

To access related items (such as activities, memory verse posters and translated texts) please visit our web store at shop.biblevisuals.org and enter 5582 in the search box on the page.

FREE TEXT DOWNLOAD

To access a FREE printable copy of the teaching text (PDF format) in English or other available languages, enter S5582DL in the search box. Add the item to your cart, and use coupon code XTACSV17 at checkout. Once your order is processed you will receive an email with a link to the free download.

South America

Venezuela
Trinidad and Tobago
Guyana
French Guiana
Colombia
Suriname
Peru
Brazil
Bolivia
Paraguay
Chile
Uruguay
Argentina

ECUADOR

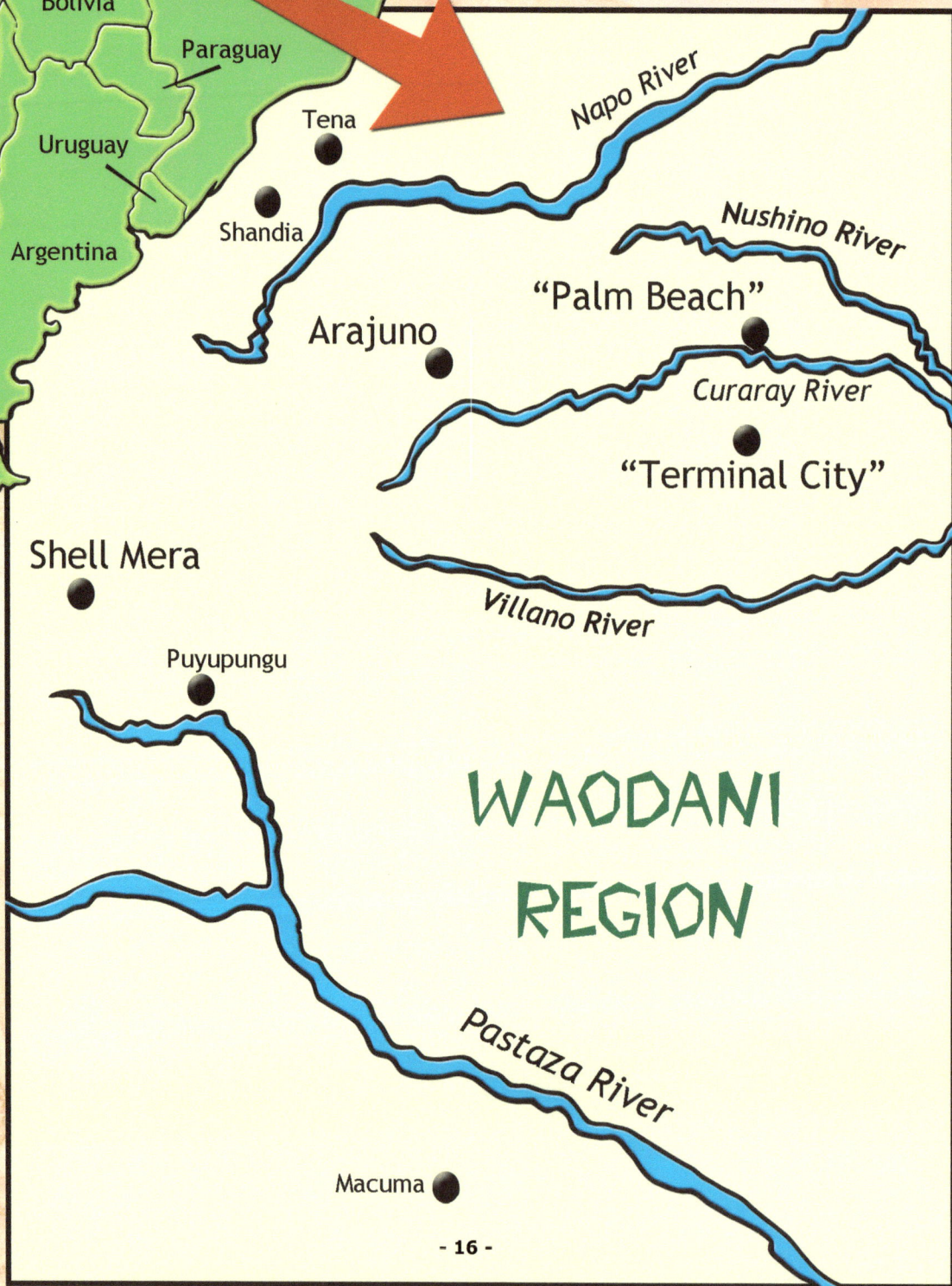

Napo River

Tena

Nushino River

Shandia

"Palm Beach"

Arajuno

Curaray River

"Terminal City"

Shell Mera

Villano River

Puyupungu

WAODANI

REGION

Pastaza River

Macuma

A man's heart deviseth his way: but the LORD directeth his steps.

Proverbs 16:9

Introduction
by Edie Cunningham

GLOSSARY

Airstrip	a dirt or grass runway for small airplanes	Ridge	a long, narrow hill
Going places	lavatory/restroom	To see [something] well	to approve of
GPS	Global Positioning System, device used for navigation	*Waengongi*	God
Itota	Jesus	*Waengongi's* house	church building
Plantain drink	a beverage similar to bananas mashed in warm water	*Waengongi's* place	Heaven
		Wao-Tededo	the Waodani language
		Wood bee	airplane

PRONUNCIATION GUIDE
Place stress on syllables in bold italic.

Babae = Bah-**bă**	Gimade = Gee-**mah**-deh	Tementa = Teh-**men**-tah
Cawaena = Kah-**wă**-nah	Itota = Ee-**toh**-tah	Paa = Pah'-ah
Coba = **Ko**-bah	Mincaye = Min-**kah**-yee	Tidi = **Tee**-dee
Curaray = Koo-**rrah**-rrie	Namo = **Nah**-moe	Tiwaeno = Tee-**wă**-no
Damointado= Dah-moin-**tah**-doh	Nampa = **Nahm**-pah	Toñae = Toe-**nyă**
Dayumae = Die-**u**-mă	Nemo = **Neh**-moe	Toñampade = Toe-nyăm-**pah**-deh
Dawa = **Dow**-wah	Nemompade= Neh-moem-**pah**-deh	
Dyuwi = Doo-**wee**	Nenkiwi = Nen-**kee**-wee	Waengongi = Wang-**ong**-ee
Epa = **Eh**-pah	Omaka = O-**mah**-kah	Waodani = Wow-dah-**nee**
Gikita = Gee-**kee**-tah	Omene = O-**meh**-neh	Wimanae = Wih-**mah**-nă

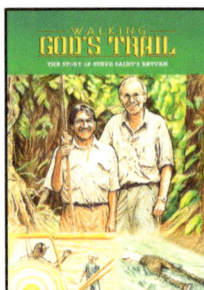

Show Front Cover

These men look as different from one another as night and day. Yet they belong to the same family. (*Teacher:* Point to Steve and *Mincaye* on the front cover.)

Can you name their differences? *(Dark hair. Blonde hair. Golden brown skin. White skin.)* But those differences are only on the *outside,* aren't they? So who *are* these men?

Steve and Mincaye are two very different men, yet they belong to the same family because they love the same God. The events that made them part of that family–that united them– really should have divided them. Why didn't that happen? The answer can be found as we travel back in time to a place deep in the Ecuadorian jungle when Steve was just a boy of five.

The Saint Family/Why They Came

Steve was a playful MK *(missionary kid)* with a toy truck made of wood and a western cowboy hat plunked on his head. He lived on the edge of a jungle in Ecuador, South America. His father, Nate Saint, was one clever jungle pilot. His mom, Marj Saint, was a tenderhearted nurse. Steve had a baby brother named Phil and an older sister named Kathy. The Saint family had moved to Ecuador as missionaries.

How They Did Their Work

Every day when Steve's dad warmed the engine of the mission plane called *56 Henry,* Steve's legs raced to keep pace with that bright yellow Piper Cub as it zipped down the airstrip and headed for the sky.

"I'll radio in later," his dad always promised.

Back in the kitchen of their jungle home at Shell Mera, Marj Saint kept the two-way radio humming. Late each afternoon, crackling sounds would signal Nate making contact. Soon his voice would break through with a few words to let Marj know he was on his way home for dinner.

Goal to Reach the Waodani

Steve's dad and four other missionary friends were very concerned about the Waodani people hidden deep in the jungle. Tribal revenge killings and disease had nearly wiped out these people. If someone didn't reach them with the good news of Jesus, they would soon be extinct. As a missionary pilot, Steve's dad spent many hours flying over the thick jungle, searching for the Waodani and their huts.

Contact with the Waodani

Finally one day Nate's excited voice broke the silence of the two-way radio: "Marj, we have contact! Over and out." Marj knew that Nate had just had his first aerial sighting of the Waodani.

For 13 weeks Nate flew over that area and dropped gifts to the Waodani using a novel bucket drop method he'd invented. Once the Waodani took out the weekly gift and put a parrot in the bucket. Nate gave it to Steve, and it became his pet.

Nate and the four missionary friends began planning for a daring face-to-face contact with these Waodani, who were considered one of the most dangerous tribes on earth. The five men collected useful information from Dayumae, a young Waodani woman who had fled from her tribe and befriended Steve's Aunt Rachel, another missionary.

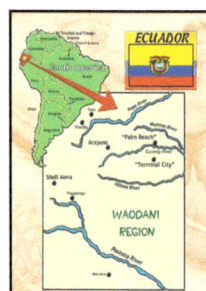

Landing on Palm Beach (Show Map)

On Tuesday, January 3, 1956, Nate Saint, Jim Elliot, Ed McCully, Pete Fleming and Roger Youderian took off in the *56 Henry.*

"It's going to be a tight landing, guys," Nate called to his friends as their yellow plane dropped out of the sky and touched down on the short sandbar along the Curaray River.

It was Friday before several Waodani cautiously stepped out of the jungle. But they did not hurry to the river's edge where the missionaries waited. Waodani were masters of the jungle, but were afraid of foreigners, and rightly so, because foreigners had always come to take, never to give.

To communicate friendship to the Waodani, whose language they didn't know, Nate, Jim, Ed, Pete and Roger shared food and used hand-motions to talk with the Waodani. One Waodani stroked the yellow "wood bee" that had fallen out of the sky. Another used his hands to beg for a ride. That night, still another Waodani slept on the sand below the missionaries' tree house.

What the five missionaries didn't know, however, was that deep in the jungle, an argument had erupted. One Waodani man had been insulted by another. Since Waodani knew no other way to settle the argument than to kill, those "foreigners" on the beach had been selected as the ones to die. Although no Waodani appeared on Saturday, when they returned to the sandbar on Sunday morning, it was with spears.

Swish, a Waodani spear cut through the air . . . and another . . . and another. Skilled marksmen and hunters, their pointed spears hit the intended targets: Nate, Jim, Ed, Pete, and Roger. Machetes finished the job. Even the yellow *56 Henry* was shredded.

Rescue Effort and Reality

On Sunday evening, Steve's mother Marj received no radio message from her husband Nate. The next day a search and rescue party was organized and sent out. What they found confirmed what they had feared. The five missionaries had been speared by the Waodani, their bodies dumped in the Curaray River.

Marj Saint, huddled together with her three children in their jungle home, prayed and cried with the other missionary families who also had lost their husbands and fathers.

It was January 8, 1956, just 22 days before Steve's fifth birthday. His dad was taken out of this life by the very people Nate had wanted to reach for Jesus. His dad's death was difficult for such a young boy to understand. Yet Steve did accept it with the help of his mother.

Was Marj Saint filled with revenge and a get-even kind of hate? No, because she knew about forgiveness. She, too, had once been God's enemy, but she had received Christ's forgiveness. His love filled her heart. Steve never once heard his mom speak against the Waodani.

Steve's Aunt Rachel and Elisabeth, Jim Elliot's widow, slowly befriended the Waodani and were invited to move into the jungle to live with the tribe. Eventually, Mincaye, the warrior who had helped to kill Steve's father and had threatened to spear Aunt Rachel, came to her hut one night and asked, "Would *Waengongi,* the Creator God, clean *anyone's* heart?" She promised that He would. Mincaye left but returned the next morning to say that he, too, had a clean heart.

Now that God had cleaned his heart, Mincaye made a promise to Aunt Rachel. Since he had been among those that had killed Steve's father, he would be the one to teach Steve how to live. Mincaye meant that he would become Steve's "father."

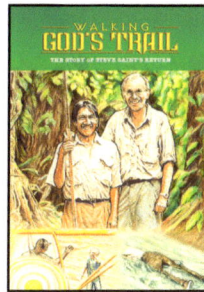

Ending (Show Front Cover)

This is Steve Saint today with his "father" Mincaye. They are both in God's family.

When Nate, Jim, Ed, Pete and Roger gave their lives for Jesus on that jungle sandbar, they had no way of knowing that they were writing the first chapter of a powerful story. We want you to hear the rest of the story of those who are now *Walking God's Trail.*

Chapter 1

Show Illustration #1

"Almost there!" called out the Waodani man poling the dugout canoe through a sharp bend in Ecuador's Curaray River.

Steve Saint rose to his feet and leaned forward. He shielded his eyes from the glaring tropical sun. He was eager to see what the Waodani had found while they were fishing and hunting for turtle eggs.

"There!" the Waodani man pointed.

One look and Steve jumped out of the canoe. He ran through the shallow water and up onto the sandbar. Before him was a jumble of rusty tubes and cables. He reached out and touched what looked like a long brown lever. *The joystick.* His mind and heart raced at the discovery.

"Pop, is this really it?" Steve's son, Jaime, asked as he ran across the sand. "Are these parts from the same airplane that's in those old photos back home?"

"Yes," said Steve. "This was my dad's plane when he was a missionary pilot here in the Amazon jungle 38 years ago."

Show Illustration #2

Steve pressed on the rusty brake and a drop of black fluid seeped out. *Thirty-eight years,* he thought with a twinge of pain deep within himself. He had been almost five years old when his dad's bright yellow plane had lifted off the mission runway and rolled to its final stop on this remote jungle sandbar where he now stood.

Unlike the previous flights into the rain forest, that time the plane never brought back his dad, Nate Saint, and his four missionary friends, Jim, Ed, Pete and Roger. When the plane failed to return, a search party found the men floating in the river, speared to death by Waodani warriors with whom they had tried to share the good news of Jesus.

Steve fingered the remains of the once bright yellow Piper Cub, the plane called *56 Henry,* which had taken his dad out of his life forever. He breathed a short prayer, and the God who had become Steve's Saviour when he was a child comforted him once again. (*Teacher*: See 2 Corinthians 1:3-7, 20.)

Growing up without a father had sometimes been hard, but Steve had found some Waodani men he could look up to –warriors whose hearts had been changed. Steve's Aunt Rachel had obeyed the call of God to go into the jungle and teach the Waodani how to walk God's trail.

Mincaye, one of the men who had killed Steve's dad, amazingly had become like a father to Steve after the murder. Mincaye had given Steve the tribal name *Babae* and had taught him to do things other Waodani boys did–like string a hammock, track wild pigs and use a blowgun to hunt monkeys.

"Does *Babae* want this?" a young voice interrupted Steve's thoughts. He looked up as a Waodani boy held out a shiny piece of aluminum he had found in the river. Steve gazed at the single word *Piper* on the metal plate and knew he was holding a miracle. It was the nameplate from his dad's plane!

"Why hasn't the river washed this nameplate away?" Jaime asked his dad.

"I . . . don't . . . know," Steve replied thoughtfully. "This light piece of metal should have been carried down to the Amazon River and out to the Atlantic Ocean at least three decades ago. God must be up to something . . . but *what*?"

After returning to the States, Steve thought about this experience for months. When Aunt Rachel, a missionary Bible translator with the Waodani, died, Steve made another trip back to the jungle village of Toñampade near Palm Beach.

Show Illustration #3

After Aunt Rachel's funeral and burial, one of the Waodani men handed Steve a blowgun and pointed to a dead bird hanging from a tree branch. *I haven't done this for a very long time,* Steve thought as he inserted the dart and raised the hollow nine-foot tube to his mouth. But there was no way to back out of the challenge; so Steve took a deep breath and puffed out his cheeks. Then, with all his might, he blew.

"He hit it! He hit it!" Mincaye shouted, jumping up and down. Steve was more surprised than anyone. He handed the blowgun back to its owner. "What about you?" he asked smiling as he moved to join the Waodani in Dayumae's cooking hut for a meal of wild pig and manioc.

When everyone had eaten, Mincaye stood up and spoke. "Many years ago *Babae's* father, Nate Saint, came flying a giant yellow wood bee. He brought gifts and wanted to speak to us about *Waengongi* the Creator God. But somebody told a lie about the missionaries. Living angry and afraid, we speared them by the river."

Steve listened with great intensity.

"Then *Babae's* Aunt Rachel came. We called her *Nemo.* She brought *Waengongi's* carvings, the Bible, and showed us how to live well. Now Nemo has gone to *Waengongi's* place and we have buried her today. Now we must teach our young people to live well. Learning the ways of the good foreigners and how to use tools and medicine, we will do this. Who will teach us to do these things for ourselves? Who will help us so that many people will walk *Waengongi's* trail?" (*Teacher:* See Deuteronomy 6:5-9.)

Show Illustration #4

When Mincaye sat down, Steve realized that everyone was staring at him. Finally, Dawa, Steve's tribal grandmother, blurted out, "Now *Babae,* we say you come and live with us."

Steve's head was spinning. *Did I really just hear that?* he thought. "Well," he said carefully, "you can send a message whenever you need me. Then I'll come and visit."

Dawa shook her finger at Steve and scolded him, "*Babae! Babae!* You are not hearing us well. We say bring your family. Come live with us as part of our tribe. What do you say?"

Steve looked out at the big green leaves of the lush rain forest and wished he could run and hide there. He had spent the last twenty-some years building a life in the United States. He owned a business in Florida and his family was comfortable there. What would his wife, Ginny, think about moving to the jungle?

"I'll speak with God and with my family," Steve offered slowly. "If God and my family see it well, then we will come."

Dawa smiled. "Having already spoken with *Waengongi,* I know He sees it well."

Steve felt as though he had to get out of Toñampade and talk about something else; so he decided to hike through the jungle to tell the old warrior Gikita that Aunt Rachel had died.

Steve asked Mincaye to go with him. He thought to himself: *Now that Mincaye's an old man, I'll finally be able to keep up with him.* But by the time they got to the top of the first steep ridge, Steve's out-of-shape muscles were aching.

"Mincaye," he panted, "can you please carry my pack?"

When they finally arrived at Gikita's hut, Steve was exhausted. He collapsed onto Gikita's hammock and quickly drank a gourd of plantain drink. When he caught his breath, he told Gikita about Aunt Rachel's death and funeral. The old warrior sat in silence before he spoke.

"Being old, I too will die soon. I say now you come and help us teach our young people to live well. Did we not teach you to walk *Waengongi's* trail as a young one? Did we not protect you and keep you safe?"

Not you, too! Steve complained inside. *And what do old warriors like Gikita and Mincaye need to be protected from?*

On the hike back through the jungle, Steve heard a plane land up ahead of them in Toñampade. He didn't want to miss his flight, so he hurried to the airstrip. But the plane wasn't for him; it had brought a load of tourists.

"What are you doing here?" Steve asked the tourists.

"We're here to see the place where a savage jungle tribe killed the five missionaries many years ago," they said excitedly. "That's one of them right there," they said, pointing to Mincaye. Immediately Steve became so angry that he could feel his face getting red. He thought, *Nobody should be allowed to come and treat my jungle family like that. Maybe the Waodani really do need my help.*

Show Illustration #5

After Steve returned to Florida, he knew he had to talk with his family about what the Waodani had asked. But just as Steve was about to gather his family together, he heard a scream from the living room. Rushing down the hall, he found his daughter Stephenie standing on the sofa holding one hand over her mouth and frantically waving the other in the air.

Crawling across the carpet was a big, ugly cockroach, the kind that invades the palm trees in Florida and slips into people's homes. Shaun, Jaime and Jesse had also heard their sister scream and were trying to pounce on the brown, shiny bug. *Oh no*, Steve worried, *how will Stephenie and the boys react to the possibility of moving to a place with cockroaches*

as big as your hand, giant tarantulas and vampire bats that try to nibble on your toes while you're asleep?

Steve took a deep breath and shared the Waodani's request with his family.

"All right, let's do it!" shouted Jesse.

"Yeah!" cried Shaun and Jaime.

What shocked Steve, however, was that Stephenie immediately jumped up and down and clapped her hands begging, "Yes, yes, Papa! Promise me we'll go. Life here is soooo boring!"

However, Steve could still see fear in Ginny's eyes. He was certain he knew what she was thinking: *How will I be a good mother in a place I don't understand – a place without doctors' offices, grocery stores, running water, or telephones? How will I keep milk cold without a refrigerator or do the laundry without a washing machine?*

Before deciding to move their family to the jungle to live with the Waodani, Steve and Ginny went on a test run. They flew to Ecuador and spent a few days with the Waodani.

While visiting the jungle, Ginny was overwhelmed at the thought of leaving behind all the things she used every day and being a mom in a place she didn't understand. But something else troubled her, too. "What could *I* do to serve the Waodani, Steve?" she asked.

God answered Ginny's nagging question one night. She sat in *Waengongi's* house and listened to the Waodani belting out the words of the kids' chorus she'd just taught them: "Pharaoh, Pharaoh, oooh baby, let my people go." The Waodani pleaded for more songs, and Ginny sang one after another in her beautiful voice.

Later that night Ginny smiled at her husband and said, "Steve, I've discovered one little thing I might be able to do for the Waodani. I can teach them to sing. I'm still uneasy about living in the jungle, but I'm starting to believe that this is the trail God has marked for our lives. When you found your dad's plane after 38 years and brought home that little Piper nameplate, I knew something was going to happen. I didn't know what it was then, but now I know. God wants us to move to the jungle. Let's trust Him and follow wherever that trail leads."

APPLICATION

Read Proverbs 3:5-6. Do you trust in yourself or in the Creator God who made you? Sometimes God has surprise plans for us that can turn our world upside down! These can be challenging times, but they often help us learn to trust Him with our whole life.

Chapter 2

This could be a big problem, thought Steve Saint as he walked slowly out of the hanger and toward the airstrip in Shell Mera, Ecuador. *I thought at least* one *pilot here would have a GPS I could use. Now how am I going to navigate through the jungle and find a good spot for our new home and the Waodani tribal center?*

Suddenly, a stranger walked up and asked abruptly, "Do you love Jesus?"

Steve looked up at the tall, bearded man. "Well . . . yes, I

do," he said.

The man smiled, "Looking for a GPS? The name's Rick . . . and I have one you could use."

Steve opened his mouth to say something, but the stranger kept talking. "I use it when I'm flying my plane in the jungle. Would you like to see my plane?"

"Sure," Steve said and followed Rick down an old dirt road to a hangar where a small plane was kept.

Show Illustration #6

"This airplane's name is *Bravo Tango Sierra*," Rick said, "but I just call her *BTS* for short."

Suddenly Rick's eyes lit up. "I've been praying that God would send someone to look after *BTS* for a while," he said. "Would you be able to use a plane?"

Being a pilot also, Steve knew how useful an airplane like this would be in the jungle. *Wow!* He thought. *I didn't even think I'd find a GPS, and now I'm offered a plane!* He felt a little foolish for having been so worried. God was planning ahead, and He could make impossible things possible! (*Teacher:* See Matthew 19:26.)

Steve took Rick's GPS and some maps of the jungle and went back to the village of Toñampade. Together, he and the Waodani studied the maps for a place which offered the easiest trails to and from the most villages.

Finally, Coba, one of Steve's childhood Waodani friends, stabbed one map with his finger. "I see this place well," he said. "Hiking from village to village, we'll be there in several days."

Several days! Steve groaned as he remembered the painful hike to Gikita's hut and back. But he reminded himself that these Waodani knew the jungle. So before long, he and three Waodani guides were hacking through thick vines and branches, climbing ridges as tall as the Washington Monument, and sloshing across jungle streams. Along the way they met people from different Waodani villages, including some Waodani hunters who were looking for a jaguar and a girl who had been poisoned by the barb on a stingray's tail.

Later they ate tapir meat at the hut of Omene, another of Steve's old friends, who told them a sad story about his son. "A scorpion stung my son's foot and it became cold," he said. "Then his whole leg became cold. When the cold reached here, (Omene pointed to Steve's heart) he was no more. Having no medicine, we could not save him. I buried my son over there." The story was difficult for Steve to absorb. These people had no medical help for emergencies.

After several exhausting days on the trail, Coba announced, "We have reached the good dirt."

"But how do you know this is the place?" Steve panted, wiping the sweat from his forehead. "It looks just like the rest of the jungle." Curious, Steve got out his map and GPS and, sure enough, without a map or compass, Coba had led them to the exact spot he had pointed to on the map. Here they would build an airstrip for the plane and Steve's new home.

Steve made a quick trip to the United States to gather supplies for the airstrip construction project in Ecuador. When it was time to stand in line at the airport to fly back to Ecuador, he worried about check-in regulations. Getting clearance for his 600-pound pile of luggage could be a problem.

"Next," said a serious looking ticket agent named Connie, who was standing behind the counter. "And just where do you think you're going with all this stuff?" she demanded.

"The . . . Amazon jungle . . . ," Steve started to explain.

"The Amazon!" the agent gasped. "I've always wanted to see the Amazon." Then, after holding up other customers to learn about Steve's plans, Connie made an offer: "I'll let you take all this stuff if I can come visit you."

Steve was shocked. But looking at her face, he could tell she was serious.

"Sure!" he replied. "It's a deal!"

At the airstrip construction site in Ecuador, the Waodani quickly cleared dozens of trees and leveled the dirt. Steve and just his three sons headed into Nemompade and camped on the jungle floor. Together they worked on turning trees into boards to build a jungle home for the entire family.

One morning Steve woke them up early. "Shaun, Jaime, Jesse! Today your mother and sister are coming!" he said excitedly. "They'll be here in a few hours."

The three boys popped awake and looked at the house. There was no kitchen, no bathroom, no running water and no electricity. It looked like a tent without walls.

Show Illustration #7

When Ginny and Stephenie appeared in the clearing, all eyes turned toward the older woman. She put her hands on her hips as she looked around. "It's beautiful," she said. "I love it." Ginny soon became a great jungle mom. She did the family laundry down at the river and prepared tasty meals of turtle eggs, exotic birds, and monkey meat. (*Teacher:* See Philippians 4:11-13.)

One day a Waodani hunter brought her a gift, a large catfish with its insides hanging out. Ginny smiled politely, while she squirmed inside thinking, *How do I get that ready for the cooking pot?* Seeing the nervous look on Ginny's face, Marga, a Waodani woman, slung the whole thing over her shoulder and slipped away. A little while later she returned with clean filets neatly wrapped in banana leaves.

Early one morning later on, when Marga's daughter handed Steve something wrapped in cloth, he thought it felt like another fish or piece of meat. But when he set it down on the sink, the soft bundle made a crying sound. Steve lifted the cloth, peeked, and then exclaimed softly, "Ginny, Stephenie . . . Marga has given us her newborn baby!"

Ginny knew Marga intended the baby to tie them together for life. Although Ecuadorian law would not permit adoption, the Saints became "co-parents." Ginny and Stephenie named the newborn Ana Beth before returning her to Marga's arms.

Stephenie loved having a little Waodani "sister" and playing with Waodani children. She and Jesse even started a school to teach them about the world outside the jungle. And Stephenie also took charge of the Saints' unusual pets: a broken-winged macaw, two monkeys, and a wild pig that thought it was a dog and liked to chase chickens!

Jesse developed a special bond with his adopted grandfather, Mincaye. The Saints had become part of the Waodani tribe.

Show Illustration #8

One evening when "Grandpa" Mincaye fell asleep on one of the Saints' hammocks, Jesse sneaked up and tied a string through the decorative hole in Mincaye's earlobe. Then Jesse ran the string behind the hammock and tied it through the big hole in Mincaye's other ear. Everyone watched to see what Jesse would do next. Teasingly, he shook Mincaye awake, whispering loudly, "Mincaye, night monkeys! Let's go hunt them and eat them."

Mincaye jumped up and headed for the door, but he didn't get very far before the string tightened. He fell backwards into the hammock, swinging wildly and yelling. Everyone exploded into laughter.

Show Illustration #9

But life was not all fun. Before long, more than one Waodani village knew that *Babae* and his family had brought a "wood bee" to the jungle. Steve loved flying the airplane from village to village for them, but soon that was all he was doing. So he asked the Waodani God-followers, "Will the tribal elders please tell me which flights are more important?" (*Teacher:* See Exodus 18:13-24.)

They looked at each other and shrugged their shoulders. Nobody even seemed to know who the "elders" were. "I can't tell you what is best for you," said Steve. "Some of you will have to make choices for the whole community, like when to build your clinic and when to build your school. And you will need to get money to do these things." Eventually, the Waodani realized Steve was speaking well, so they called a big meeting and selected nine Waodani elders or leaders.

One day, as Steve sat in a Waodani elder meeting, he saw their pet wild pig walk by with chicken feathers in its mouth and what looked like a grin on its face. Steve shook his head and frowned at the pig.

Show Illustration #10

After the meeting, Ginny took Steve aside. She looked very serious. "Steve," she asked, "did you see what happened in the meeting when our pet pig walked by?"

"Yes," said Steve, "that crazy pig has been chasing the chickens again!"

"Yes, I know, but that's not what I'm talking about," Ginny said. "You were looking at the pig, so you frowned. But all the elders were looking at you. When they saw you frown, they thought you didn't like a decision they had made, so they changed their minds." Frustrated, Ginny started to cry.

Oh, no, Steve thought. *The Waodani elders are trying to make only those decisions that make me happy.* The only way for the Waodani to start doing things on their own was for them to decide things without Steve.

"We're going to have to leave our jungle home," moaned Steve, "but I don't think I can go back to being a businessman." Steve buried his face in his hands. "God, where's your trail leading now?" he prayed. (*Teacher:* See Proverbs 16:9 and 19:21.)

Before the Saints moved back to the United States, Steve asked Waodani elders to help him baptize Shaun, Jesse and Stephenie, just as the Waodani had baptized him as a young boy. Before Grandfather Mincaye baptized Jesse, he said, "You go on God's trail. Don't go over here or there; just keep always, always following God's trail."

APPLICATION:

Have you begun to walk God's trail? The trail starts at the cross where Jesus died for your sin. Isn't it time you tell God that you agree with Him about your sin and thank Him for sending Jesus to die for you on the cross? Will you remain behind today so that I can help you, like Mincaye, like Jesse, begin walking God's trail?

Chapter 3

At home in Florida, Steve Saint picked up his journal and flipped through pages of his jungle adventures. He sighed as he read, "Each day back in the United States makes me miss jungle life with my Waodani family even more. I wonder if anything meaningful will ever fill these blank pages."

Then the phone rang. It was his mother, Marj. "Steve, I came across some old reels of movie film. I'd like to know what's on them, but I can't get the projector to work. Can you come over?"

Show Illustration #11

After Steve got to his mom's house and tinkered with the projector, he started to play the first reel of movie film. He and his mother watched old footage of his dad flying *56 Henry* in the jungle.

"I've seen this before," he said, "but that frame in the film copy cut off just as the plane is about to land. I've always wondered if Dad really landed on that very short sandbar or whether he was just flying low for the camera."

This time, though, Steve saw his dad complete the difficult landing. "Dad really did it!" Steve exclaimed excitedly. Without any doubt he knew his dad had been a very good pilot.

Show Illustration #12

Two months later, Steve returned to check on the Waodani. But when he stepped off the plane, nobody in the group at the airstrip came running to greet him. Everyone just stood quietly. *Oh no!* Steve wondered. *Has somebody died?* Finally everyone came together and sat down.

Mincaye spoke first: "Many years ago *Babae's* father came flying in a yellow wood bee. Then many years later another wood bee came, and in that wood bee was *Babae* himself. He took the elders from place to place to teach people, and he carried medicine for the sick. But what about now? *Babae* has left and we have no wood bee. *Babae*, we think we need our own wood bee. What do you think?"

This idea is crazy, Steve thought. *These Waodani still kill their dinner with a spear and sleep in thatch-roofed huts. How could they buy and fly an airplane?* Steve chose his words carefully: "If God sees it is well, then maybe someday you will have a Waodani plane and a Waodani pilot."

Quickly, they replied, "Having already spoken with *Waengongi*, we have chosen Tementa to be our pilot. Now we need a wood bee!"

"It takes *nangi, nangi, nangi tucudi* to buy an airplane," Steve said.

"You showing us what to do, we will work very hard and save lots of money," they responded.

Show Illustration #13

While flying out of the jungle,

Steve had to make an unscheduled landing because of bad weather. While waiting at the airstrip in Tena, he noticed an unusual lightweight aircraft parked on the airstrip. When he went over to investigate, the owner offered to take him for a ride.

As they flew, the man explained, "It's not very fancy, but it's cheap and easy to maintain. It's not all that fast, but I can fly and I don't even have a license."

Steve looked over the shoulder of the unlicensed pilot, then at the ground far below. "Uh . . . " he began. "Let's go down now."

Steve had seen all he needed to see. This type of plane would be perfect for the Waodani. When he returned to the United States, Steve gathered parts and worked on plans for the first all-Waodani aircraft—their own wood bee!

The Waodani paid for the plane parts with money they earned by giving "real experience tours." These were designed for foreigners, like Connie the ticket agent, who had always wanted to see the jungle for themselves.

News that Steve was helping the Waodani put together their own plane in Ecuador spread quickly. Soon other jungle tribes came by to watch.

"Will you show us how to build our own plane too?" they asked Steve.

"I'm sorry," he replied, "I am much too busy helping with this plane."

But when the Waodani heard what Steve had said to the other tribes, they scolded him. "*Babae*, you do not have time, but we do. Maybe we can teach the other tribes to build wood bees and use medicine. And while doing this, we can teach them to walk *Waengongi's* trail." (*Teacher:* See Matthew 28:19-20.)

That night Steve lay awake thinking. All kinds of ideas began to swirl around in his mind. He decided that when he got back to Florida, he would start a ministry called I-TEC to make the Waodani's wish come true. He'd help them take care of their own medical and dental needs and simplify tools to fit their jungle ways of thinking and living. Then they could pass the same methods and tools on to other tribes. Perhaps through the Waodani many would begin to walk God's trail and know Jesus as their Saviour.

After a year back home in the United States, Jesse and Stephenie begged Steve to bring Grandfather Mincaye to Florida for Jesse's high school graduation and Jaime's wedding.

Steve liked the idea, but there were two big problems. Mincaye didn't have a passport or other special papers to allow his entrance into the United States. And there was only one day left of Steve's trip to test the Waodani's new plane. There was no way he could get those papers for Mincaye.

Still Steve decided to travel to the U.S. Embassy in Quito with Mincaye, fill out one of Mincaye's forms, and go to the back of a long line. *This will never work*, he thought.

When one of the officials saw what Steve had written, he laughed. "Look at this," he called to his co-workers. "This man named Mincaye lives in the jungle and his job is a hunter/gatherer!"

Then, though Steve wasn't told why, he and Mincaye were bumped to the front of the line and Mincaye's papers were signed! The rest of that busy day, the same thing happened at several other places, and soon Mincaye was on a giant wood bee, a 757 aircraft, headed for the United States!

Show Illustration #14

Mincaye was fascinated by the world outside the jungle. On Mincaye's first day in Florida, Steve took him to a grocery store. When they got inside, Mincaye asked, "*Babae*, whose food is all this?"

"It is for everyone," Steve said.

"Then if I ever have to move out of the jungle, I want to live in one of these food houses," he said. "Hunting is easy in this place!"

Some time later, Mincaye was in Florida for a special welcome home party for Stephenie, who had spent one year on a missions trip. Not long after the party began, Stephenie tapped Steve on the shoulder. She was holding her forehead.

"Pop, I have a headache," she explained. "I'm going to go lie down for a while."

A few minutes later, Steve found her holding her head with both hands. Then, while Steve and Ginny prayed for her, she let out a cry of pain and her eyes rolled back into her head. Steve whipped out his cell phone and frantically dialed 9-1-1. At the hospital they learned that, although they couldn't see it, Stephenie's brain was bleeding and she was dying.

Steve and Mincaye watched helplessly as emergency staff crowded around her and stuck her full of tubes and needles.

"*Babae*, who is doing this thing?" Mincaye demanded, glaring at the emergency staff. Mincaye hadn't forgotten how to be a warrior, and Steve feared Mincaye might even try to help him defend Stephenie.

"No one is doing this," said Steve. "I don't know what's happening." However, even though Stephenie never regained consciousness and died, the anger slowly left Mincaye's face, and he started to smile.

"*Babae*, now I see this well. *Waengongi* is doing this. He is taking Stephenie to His place to be with Him. Being old, soon I will go there too. Don't be sad, *Babae*. Doesn't *Waengongi* know all things? Doesn't He do all things well?" (*Teacher:* See Jeremiah 29:11.)

The day after Stephenie's funeral, even though they were still very sad, Steve, Mincaye and Tementa flew to Europe for a large missionary conference in Amsterdam. They had been asked to come and share their experiences with other God-followers from all around the world.

Show Illustration #15

As the three men walked up onto the platform and looked out at the huge international crowd of 11,000 people, Mincaye whispered to Steve, "I see this well. Many people from all over the dirt, all walking *Waengongi's* trail."

Steve introduced the first Waodani pilot, Tementa, who waved to the cheering crowd. Then Steve handed the microphone to Mincaye.

"Long ago," the old warrior began, "we acted badly, hating and killing. When *Babae's* father came in a yellow wood bee, we speared him."

The crowd was silent.

Mincaye continued, "Then *Babae's* Aunt Rachel came and brought us *Waengongi's* carvings. We learned of *Waengongi's* Son who died to wash our hearts clean. Now we live well. Speaking *Waengongi's* carvings all over the world, let's take many people with us to *Waengongi's* place."

The crowd erupted with applause. Finally, Steve shouted, "Thank you!" into the microphone and added, "There is one more thing I want to say. When Mincaye and the other Waodani warriors killed my father, they meant it for evil. But if you have heard the story of my father's death before, and God has used it to do something good in your life, please stand."

Steve was hoping that at least a few people would stand up and wave, but that's not what happened. All across the auditorium, thousands of people stood to their feet.

"I see this very well," said Mincaye.

"I do too," said a teary-eyed Steve. "God really does all things well."

JUMPING THE BOA
A Gospel Invitation

(*Teacher:* Make a cloth boa snake. On the length of one side write the words "Sin and Death–Romans 6:23." Use the snake as you teach Mincaye's words.)

This story takes place as the Saints are preparing to move to the jungle.

The boat motor hummed steadily as Steve guided the modernized dugout canoe down the waters of the Curaray River and deep into the Amazon jungle. Mincaye and the other Waodani passengers rested lazily, but Jesse was filled with energy and curiosity. He couldn't wait to see the place where they would build their new home and begin their jungle adventure. He gazed at the colorful jungle canopy over their heads and examined the canoe that had been hollowed out of a single log.

His older brother Shaun sat beside him, carefully wiping dirt and mud from an old flight instrument that two Waodani men had found in the river and given to Steve.

"That gauge shows how high the plane is flying," Steve said, pointing to the altimeter in Shaun's hand. "Every piece of old *56 Henry* reminds me of my dad. This piece especially reminds me of how quickly and unexpectedly his life was taken."

Suddenly Jesse jumped to his feet. "Pop, look!" he cried, pointing to the steep riverbank. "Do you see it? Do you see it?"

Steve slowed the motor, then turned the canoe around and headed toward the spot. As the canoe got closer, everyone could see what Jesse was pointing at–an enormous snake on the nearby ledge.

Quickly, the Waodani scampered to the back of the canoe, but Shaun, Jesse and Steve leaned forward to get a better look.

"Wow!" Steve exclaimed. "That boa must be at least 13 feet long and ten inches around!"

(*Teacher:* Use a tape measure to show the length and a child's belt to show how round the boa was.)

Jesse grabbed a pole from the bottom of the canoe. "Pop, can I?"

When the Waodani saw what Jesse was about to do, they called out frantically, and some of them placed one foot up onto the opposite edge of the canoe.

Jesse reached out and nudged the boa with the end of the pole. Everyone held his breath. The snake barely moved. It just lay there, napping in a patch of sunlight.

As they continued on down the river, Jesse asked, "Pop, why were the Waodani so afraid of that big snake?"

Steve looked at Grandfather Mincaye, and everyone grew quiet.

Mincaye cleared his throat. "My ancestors once told a legend about the boa. Dying, a man's body goes into the dirt, and his spirit walks the afterlife trail. But what does the man find blocking the trail? The boa. Only by jumping it can the man continue on his way."

"What if he can't jump over it?" Jesse asked.

"Then he becomes a pile of termites," Mincaye answered.

The boys grew wide-eyed and then began to laugh.

Mincaye smiled, "We no longer believe all the words of the ancient legends."

Suddenly, the old warrior's face grew deeply serious.

"Now we know what really blocks each one as he walks his trail. It is more deadly than the mighty boa. It is sin, the things *Waengongi's* carvings say He does not see well. Living badly, we all do these things. These sins block our path to *Waengongi's* place. Being very strong and brave, a person might jump over a boa, but never his sin. How can anyone face this 'boa' and live?"

Shaun looked down at the altimeter in his hands. He and Jesse both knew it was Mincaye's spear that had forced their grandfather, Nate Saint, to "face the boa" many years before.

Mincaye leaned forward and placed a hand on each boy's shoulder. Then he said, "Living angry, I once did many things that *Waengongi* did not see well. But then I learned what Nate Saint had come to tell us. *Waengongi* sent His own son, *Itota* –Jesus–to jump the boa for us. *Itota* lived very well, always walking *Waengongi's* trail. But men like me nailed *Itota* to a tree. Then, *Itota* being dead three days, *Waengongi* made Him alive again. When we die, He can make us alive again too."

(*Teacher*: As you say the words "jump the boa", do just that –jump over the boa snake to make your point clear.)

Mincaye leaned back in the canoe. "How happy I am that *Waengongi* loves me and that *Itota* died for me! How happy I am that He forgave my sins and washed my heart clean. Now, believing *Waengongi's* carvings and walking His trail, I live well. One day I will go to be in *Waengongi's* place. There I will see Nate Saint, your grandfather, and all those who lived for *Itota* just as I now do. Happily we will greet each other, and

Waengongi's place will be our home forever."

"But first, we have another home to build," Steve interrupted.

He stopped the motor. And with wide eyes and big grins, Shaun and Jesse looked into the dense jungle that was now their home.

(*Teacher:* See Ephesians 2:1-10, 1 Corinthians 15:3-4, and John 14:2-3.)

Review Questions
By Bryan Willoughby

Chapter 1

1. Where do Steve Saint and his family live? *(Florida)*
2. What discovery brings Steve and his son Jaime to the jungle river? *(The finding of Steve's father's old missionary plane,)*
3. What are some of the emotions Steve experiences while examining this airplane? *(Excitement, surprise, pain, wonder)*
4. What had happened to Steve's dad? *(He and four other missionaries had been speared to death by Waodani warriors.)*
5. How long ago was Steve's dad killed? *(Thirty-eight years ago)*
6. What had happened to Mincaye to change him from an angry warrior to Steve's caring adoptive father? *(He had learned about God and His Word from Steve's Aunt Rachel and had decided to live for God.)*
7. Why do the Waodani want Steve and his family to move to the jungle? *(The Waodani want the Saints to teach them the ways of foreigners and how to use tools and medicine, so they can teach their own children to live well.)*
8. What would your reaction be if your dad or mom suddenly suggested that your family move to the jungle? *(Perhaps surprise, excitement, fear, concern about moving away from friends, etc.)*
9. What happens in the jungle that causes Steve to think that maybe the Waodani really do need his help? *(He meets some tourists who are rude to Mincaye.)*
10. What does Ginny think is a clue that God has a plan for them in the jungle? *(That Steve's dad's plane was discovered after being hidden for so long)*

Chapter 2

1. What does a stranger offer to let Steve use along with the GPS he needs? *(A small airplane)*
2. The thought of a long hike makes Steve groan. What do you think are some of the challenges involved in hiking through the jungle? *(Plants and vines blocking the trail, steep hills, streams to cross, dangerous animals and hot weather)*
3. Why wasn't Omene able to save his son when he was stung by a scorpion? *(Because he didn't have the medicine his son needed)*
4. What does Steve's Waodani guide Coba use to guide them through the jungle? *(He uses his own sense of direction and knowledge of the jungle.)*
5. The Saints' new home has no electricity or running water. What things in your house use electricity or running water and would be hard to live without? *(The toilet, refrigerator, electric lights, shower, telephones...)*
6. What are some of the unusual jungle foods that Steve and his family eat? *(Turtle eggs, exotic birds, monkey meat, catfish, tapir meat, plantain drink, wild pig and manioc)*
7. Why does Marga give her newborn baby to Ginny and Steve? *(She hopes sharing the baby will join them together in a lifelong friendship.)*

8. What does Steve become busy doing for the Waodani? *(Flying them from place to place in the airplane)*
9. Why do you think Steve wants the Waodani elders, not him, to make community decisions? *(He believes that only the Waodani can know what is best for them, and perhaps he believes that it is their responsibility to make these decisions.)*
10. Why do Steve and Ginny decide to leave the jungle and move back to Florida? *(They can see that as long as Steve is around, the elders will try to make decisions that Steve likes instead of thinking about what is best for the people.)*

Chapter 3

1. What does Steve's mother find that cheers him up? *(Some old movie film that shows Steve's dad making a difficult landing in 56 Henry)*
2. To whom did the Waodani speak about having their own airplane before they talked with Steve? *(They had prayed to God about it.)*
3. How do Steve and the Waodani work together on the Waodani aircraft project? *(Steve finds a good design for the plane and gathers parts; the Waodani come up with the idea and pay for the parts; together they assemble the plane.)*
4. What is I-TEC? *(Steve's idea for a ministry that will make high tech tools and medicine simpler–to fit the jungle lifestyle)*
5. The Waodani want to teach other jungle tribes to walk God's trail. Do you think the Waodani believers will be good missionaries? *(Perhaps yes, because they probably have a lot in common with the other tribes and will know how to share about Jesus in a way they can understand.)*
6. Why does it seem as if it will be impossible to bring Mincaye to the United States for Jaime's wedding and Jesse's graduation? *(Mincaye needs a passport and other special papers and has only one day to get them.)*
7. Mincaye has a lot of fun visiting his first grocery store in Florida. Where would you take Mincaye if he came to your town? *(Perhaps a train station, skyscraper, ski slope, bowling alley, a beach or your church)*
8. Why do you think Mincaye's frown turns into a smile, even though he knows that Stephenie is dying? *(Perhaps because he knows that Stephenie belongs to Jesus and will go to Heaven; he knows he can trust God's ways.)*
9. If Steve found a time machine and could go back in time and change his past, what if anything do you think he would change? *(He would probably change nothing, because he has seen how even sad events can be part of God's plan.)*
10. Steve's Florida-based ministry I-TEC has now helped many people around the world. If God had plans for Steve and his family in Florida, why do you think He ever sent them to the jungle? *(Perhaps he wanted them to really know how the Waodani live, or He wanted them to learn to trust Him, or perhaps He wanted to give them an adventure!)*